Better Homes a

Workshop
Projects

LEN CRANE

MINI · WORKBOOK · SERIES

MURDOCH BOOKS®
Sydney • London • Vancouver • New York

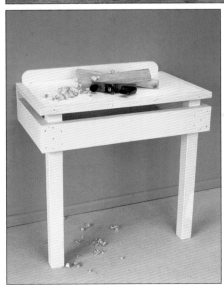

CONTENTS

Bench with storage (top), wall-mounted bench (bottom, far left) and shadow board with fold-away bench (bottom right)

A tidy, well-organised workshop is the dream of many an amateur or professional craft worker. A corner of your home or garage is all that's required.

Your workshop

You'll spend quite a lot of time in your workshop, so make an effort now to ensure that you'll be comfortable and safe while you work.

PURPOSE

The set-up of your new workshop will depend on its intended uses. Some will require a general area for basic tool storage and simple repairs around the home and garden, while others might want a special-purpose layout to cater for their hobby.

LOCATION

If you are fortunate you may have a studio, shed or garage you can dedicate to your needs or hobby. The space available will dictate the layout of your workshop, so very careful planning is necessary to make it as efficient as possible. If you are a hobbyist motor mechanic you'll require at least a one-car garage, but if you make delicate wooden miniatures, between four and six square metres in the corner of a spare room may suit you. In all cases it is important that your workshop is well organised, well lit, well ventilated, safe and easy to clean.

LIGHT AND AIR

Ventilation and light are vital and must be thought about very early in the planning stages. Cross ventilation is ideal, so if possible locate your main work space between a door and a window. If your work is dusty or you are likely to use solvents or other vaporous chemicals, cross ventilation with the air flow from your back is preferable. This, together with an appropriate face mask, will provide reasonable protection from air-borne substances. Consider fan-assisted ventilation if you are unable to get a good cross-flow of air. If you are in a cold climate where doors and windows are kept closed and the room is often heated, ensure that the air in the workshop moves around by using a fan-forced air circulating system, preferably with an easy-to-clean filter.

Windows in the south wall will supply good daylight without direct sunlight, and this is ideal for woodworking. If a window is not available, skylights that use a flexible silvered tube to direct the light are excellent alternatives and simple to install. For those times when artificial lighting is needed, 150-watt halogen floodlights are preferable: fluorescent lighting, while popular, is not a good workshop lighting system because it distorts colours and gives rise to a phenomenon called the stroboscopic effect, when a rotating part spinning very fast appears to be stationary.

This is a serious safety hazard when you are using variable speed machines, such as routers, drills and lathes.

LAYOUT

Primarily you will require a sturdy, flat work surface, such as a wooden bench or table, and sufficient space to assemble and manoeuvre your projects. If your work space will be shared with other activities, consider a folding workbench and lockable shadow board for tool storage. In a small space, a wall-mounted bench or a bench with storage underneath will be more useful. If you are lucky enough to have a large, dedicated workshop, a freestanding workbench will give you the greatest flexibility and satisfaction.

You will probably need some kind of vice fitted to your workbench, so think about where you will place it and how much clearance you will need for the type of projects you will be working on.

If you have any fixed machinery, such as a table saw, drill press or lathe, try to arrange them so that movement between the various work stations with your projects is easy and relaxed. The floor surface should be given a lot of thought, especially if you will be standing for long periods, and it should be easy to sweep and keep clean. Cover or eliminate low spaces under cupboards and shelves, where dust and dropped items can hide and be difficult to recover.

Have your tools within easy reach of your work space, each with its own place to ensure that you can always find the equipment you need. The worst place to store tools is on the 'big shelf'—that is, the floor. Most hand tools lend themselves to being stored on a shadow board, and a well-designed shadow board is a great asset in any workshop. The board can be custom-built to suit your tool collection and the available space, and there is a wide variety of purpose-made hardware to mount the tools. A narrow shelf below the shadow board, perhaps with a shallow tray for pencils and other small items, will help keep things in order. A low, open shelf under the workbench or nearby is fine for storing portable electrical tools such as a drill or circular saw. The upper limits of the tool storage area must be no higher than you can comfortably reach, and frequently used tools should be stored at bench height or above, if possible, to eliminate unnecessary bending.

The practical and convenient workshop layout shown at right was originally designed for a practitioner of fine woodwork. You may note the following points of interest:

- The shadow board with all its tools, the small drawer unit and the various shelves are all close and convenient to the workbench.
- The band saw, the most often used of the set machines, is also nearby.
- The windows are well located, giving maximum natural light; which is supplemented by several small halogen floodlights (not shown).

• The window over the set machines faces south to avoid direct sunlight.
• The area between the bench and the roller door is adequate for assembling large items.

ELECTRICAL SUPPLY

Pendant general-purpose electrical outlets are convenient and safe. Hanging above the work area, they keep the cords of portable tools away from the workbench or floor where they might accidentally be damaged or tripped over, as well as providing a greater working range for the tools. You may also need to install extra lighting, which should be placed over your work areas and aimed carefully so as to eliminate annoying shadows and dark spots.

Have your electrician provide sufficient circuit capacity for additional outlets that may become necessary later, and ask about special-purpose outlets or circuits that may be required if you intend to use machinery or welding equipment.

SAFETY

Keep your work area clean and tidy, not only so it will be a pleasant place to work, but for safety and health reasons. Always observe good working practices, such as wearing the correct safety gear and using tools for the purpose for which they were designed. Be alert and protect yourself, your family, friends, and anyone else who may have reason to enter your workshop.

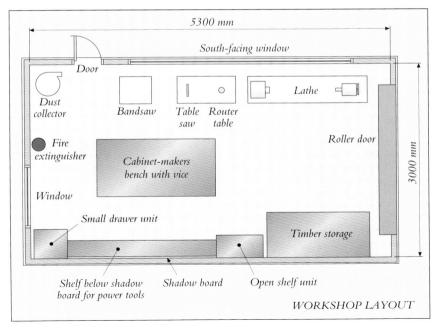

WORKSHOP LAYOUT

SAFETY EQUIPMENT

SAFETY GOGGLES
Eye protection is essential when using power tools

SAFETY MASK
A full-face mask may also be useful to protect against small flying particles

CARTRIDGE FACE MASK
More efficient than a disposable mask and ideal for working with toxic products

EAR PLUGS OR EAR MUFFS *Disposable ear plugs provide effective protection against hearing damage. Some may find ear muffs more comfortable and effective than ear plugs*

GLOVES *Provide some protection against accidental injury but must not be worn near rotating machinery*

DUST MASK
Disposable dust masks effectively keep wood dust out of the nose and mouth

WORK BOOTS
Solid shoes with non-slip soles

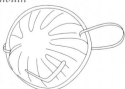

OVERALLS AND HAIRNETS *Fitted clothing helps prevent loose fabric and hair being caught in machinery*

Eye protection must be worn whenever the job requires, such as when using a router, grinder, power saw, lathe or any high-speed tool. Good ear muffs or ear plugs are essential when you are using noisy equipment: hearing damage often does not become apparent for some years after the damage is done. Disposable face masks provide sufficient protection from ordinary dust, although cartridge-type dust masks should be worn if you are working with toxic fumes or extremely fine dust. Pay attention to the manufacturer's directions when using the mask and, if your work requires the use of noxious substances, check the product label for necessary safety precautions.

Safe, comfortable footwear is a must, and protective clothing such as a pair of overalls is vital when the environment of your workplace becomes, or is likely to become, contaminated with dust or other substances. Fitted clothing and a hairnet will also help prevent loose items of clothing or hair becoming entangled in machinery.

Fixed machinery must have safety switches such as no-volt releases and emergency stop switches. No-volt releases automatically turn off the machine's on–off switch in the event of a power failure, ensuring that the machine does not start up again unexpectedly when power is restored. An emergency stop button is usually a large red knob that stops the machine when it is pressed. As an additional feature, many of these switches must be manually reset before the machine can be started again. Test these devices regularly to ensure that they will not let you down in an emergency.

If your work creates a lot of dust it would be wise to invest in a dust collection system. All wood dusts are potentially dangerous, particularly dusts from MDF and particle boards. A simple solution for a small workshop can be a domestic vacuum cleaner, but if you make a lot of dust or you work in a large area, a piped system to each machine is ideal, or you can use a mobile collector that can be wheeled about the workshop to wherever it is needed.

Press your knee against an emergency stop button to bring machinery to a quick stop.

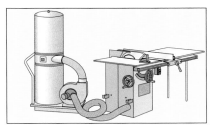

Place a small industrial dust collector with flexible hoses on a trolley and connect it to fixed machinery.

Simple wall-mounted bench

Ideal for someone who just wants to do those little maintenance jobs around the house, this structure is robust, yet requires a minimum of materials and tools to build.

TOOLS

- Builders square
- Pencil
- Tape measure or rule
- Handsaw
- Portable electric drill
- Drill bits: 5 mm, countersink, masonry bit (if required)

- Three 100 mm G-cramps
- Two 1000 mm sash cramps
- Screwdriver (cross-head)
- 300 mm wood rasp
- Spirit level

- Marking gauge
- Low-angle plane
- Hammer
- 200 mm shifting spanner (if required)
- Safety glasses
- Hearing protection
- Dust mask

CUTTING THE TIMBER

1 Take the material for the legs and mark a line all round near one end with the square and pencil, clear of any faults in the timber. From this line, measure two 862 mm lengths, allowing space for the saw cut between each length. With the handsaw, cut the legs to length, cutting on the waste side of the lines you have marked.

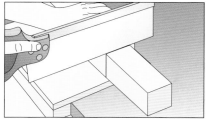

1 Use a handsaw to cut on the waste side of your marked lines for accurately measured lengths.

2 In a similar manner, mark and cut the front rail and wall cleat to 900 mm in length and each of the side rails to 560 mm.

PREPARING THE FRAME

3 Measure 20, 60 and 90 mm in from each end of the front rail and mark lines across the front face of the rail, square to the edges. On the 20 mm line, mark two screw holes 30 mm in from each edge; on the 60 mm line, mark one screw hole in the centre (69 mm) and two 15 mm in from each edge; on the 90 mm line, mark two screw holes 40 mm in from each edge. With a 5 mm drill bit and countersink bit, drill countersunk holes.

4 Measure 35 mm in from the front end of each side rail and mark a line

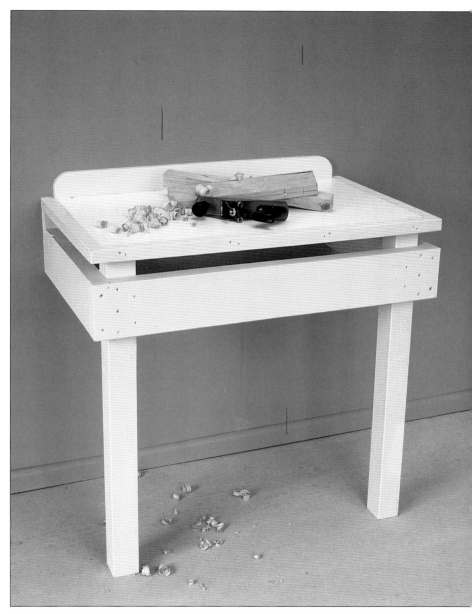

A sturdy wall-mounted workbench can make good use of a small space and requires minimal effort and materials to make.

MATERIALS★

Part	Material	Finished length	Width	No.
Leg	75 x 75 mm solid timber DAR	862 mm		2
Front rail	150 x 50 mm solid timber DAR	900 mm		1
Side rail	150 x 50 mm solid timber DAR	560 mm		2
Wall cleat	150 x 50 mm solid timber DAR	900 mm		1
Bench top	32 mm laminated MDF	840 mm	570 mm	1
Back board	75 x 31 mm solid timber DAR	840 mm		1
Lipping (front)★★	38 x 38 mm solid timber DAR	900 mm		1
Lipping (side)★★	38 x 38 mm solid timber DAR	570 mm		2

OTHER: Thirty-five 75 mm x 10 gauge wood screws; fifteen 50 mm x 10 gauge wood screws; PVA adhesive; three masonry bolts OR wall-fixing screws as required (see box on page 25).

★ Finished size: 900 x 600 mm; height 900 mm (to bench top). Timber sizes given are the nominal size. For more about timber sizes and conditions see page 17.
★★ The 38 x 38 mm lipping will give a reasonable fit, though the dressed timber will be slightly narrower than the MDF bench top. Alternatively, select 50 x 38 mm timber and dress it to the thickness of the laminated bench top, or increase the size of the MDF bench top to 900 x 600 mm and omit the lipping entirely.

on the outside face of the rail square to the edge. On this line, mark one screw hole in the centre (69 mm) and two holes 25 mm in from each edge. (Offsetting these holes from the front rail screw holes prevents the possibility of the screws meeting point to point.) Drill countersunk holes.

5 On the top of each side rail, mark a line 41 mm (or the actual thickness

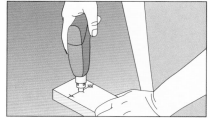

4 Use a countersink bit to ensure that the screw head will be flush with or just below the finished surface.

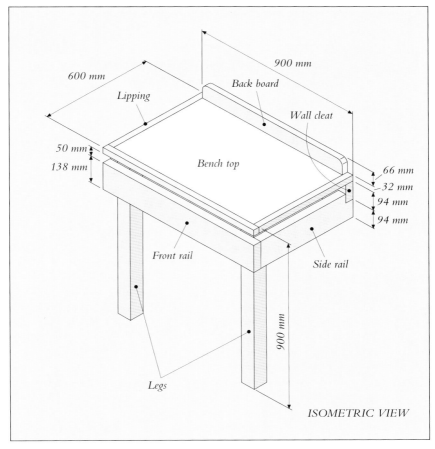

600 mm

900 mm

Lipping

Back board

Wall cleat

50 mm

138 mm

Bench top

66 mm

32 mm

94 mm

94 mm

Front rail

Side rail

900 mm

Legs

ISOMETRIC VIEW

of the wall cleat after dressing) in from the back end. With the square and pencil, continue this line onto both faces of each rail. Measure 44 mm down this line and mark a line square to it. Continue the line around onto the end of the rail and cut out the rebate with a handsaw. Mark out a rebate of the same dimensions on the bottom edge of each end of the wall cleat and cut it out in the same way. Refer to the

diagram on page 14 for a detailed view of the construction of this joint.

6 On each side rail, 20 mm down from the edge of the rebate and 20 mm in from the back end of the rail, mark and drill a countersunk hole. Similarly, mark a screw hole on the back face of the wall cleat, 20 mm up from the edge of the rebate and 20 mm in from the end of the cleat, and drill a countersunk hole.

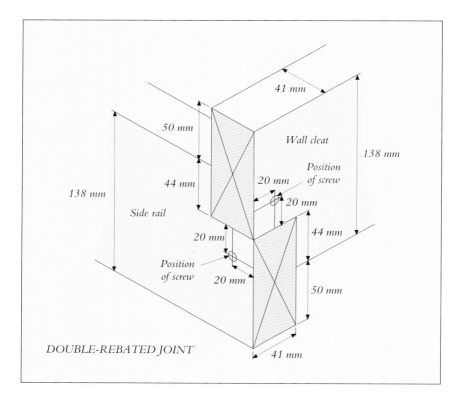

41 mm

Wall cleat

138 mm

50 mm

Position
of screw

44 mm

20 mm

20 mm

138 mm

Side rail

44 mm

20 mm

Position
of screw

20 mm

50 mm

DOUBLE-REBATED JOINT

41 mm

HINT

Use a hammer and centre punch
to mark the position of screw
holes before drilling. This helps
to prevent the drill bit wandering
across the surface.

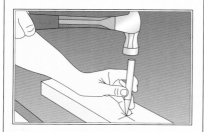

ASSEMBLING THE FRAME

7 With the square and pencil, mark a
line across two adjoining faces of
each leg, 50 mm down from the top
of the leg.

8 On the back face of the front rail,
41 mm in from each end, mark a line
square to the edge. Spread PVA
adhesive on the front face of the leg
below the line you have previously
marked, and cramp the leg to the
front rail so its outer edge is aligned
with the line you have marked on
the back face of the rail, and the top
of the rail is aligned with the line you

have marked on the leg. (A 50 mm length of the leg will be above the top of the front rail.) Insert the 75 mm x 10 gauge screws. Repeat with the other leg.

9 Spread a small amount of adhesive on the ends of each side rail and allow to dry for approximately thirty minutes. This makes a seal on the end grain which prevents it soaking up all the adhesive. Spread adhesive on the side of the leg and the back face of the front rail where it protrudes. Cramp the side rail to the leg, ensuring that it is aligned with the front rail. Make sure the housing for the wall cleat is on the upper side of the rail. Insert the screws through the side rail and from the front face of the front rail and repeat for the other side. Screws inserted into the end grain of timber won't hold securely so prevent them loosening by removing them one at a time and filling the holes with PVA adhesive before reinserting the screw.

10 Check the fit of the wall cleat on the frame and make sure it is square. Spread adhesive inside the rebates, fit the cleat, insert the 75 mm x 10 gauge screws and tighten as before.

ASSEMBLING THE TOP

11 Cut the bench top to size, if necessary. Cut the lipping to size as indicated in the materials list and set aside the longer (front) piece. Take the two side pieces and determine which is the outer face of each. Mark

a line with a marking gauge down the centre of each outer face and, on this line, mark three screw holes 30 mm in from each end and in the centre. Using a 5 mm drill bit, drill and countersink holes for the 50 mm x 10 gauge wood screws. Apply adhesive to both back faces of the lipping and use sash cramps to secure them to the side edges of the bench top, ensuring that the top of the batten is exactly level with the top of the laminate before inserting the screws to secure. Repeat the process for the front piece, with screw holes starting 60 mm from one end, then at 260 mm intervals.

12 Cut the back board to size and shape the corners if desired. To do this, use a compass or a round object such as the lid of a jar to mark the curve at either end of the back board and cut away the waste with a handsaw. Smooth over any rough edges with a rasp. Centre the back board on the back edge of the laminated bench top and mark its location. Turn the bench top over and measure three evenly spaced

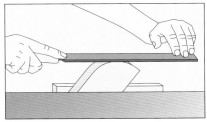

12 After cutting with a handsaw, use a rasp to reduce the corners of the back board to a rounded finish.

The 50 mm clearance between the bench top and the side rails is designed to allow the use of clamps to hold work pieces in place. Pieces may also be clamped vertically to the front and side rails.

screw holes between the marks indicating the ends of the back board and drill countersunk holes from the underside. Insert the screws and firmly screw the back board in place.

INSTALLATION

13 Select the type of wall fasteners appropriate for your wall (see box on page 25). Mark a horizontal line on the wall 862 mm above the floor. Position the frame so that the top edge of the wall cleat aligns with this line and check that the leg tops and the wall cleat are level. Lay the bench top on the legs and wall cleat and check that it is square and level.

14 Mark the locations of the holes for the wall cleat. Drill holes and

secure the frame to the wall, following steps appropriate to the type of wall fasteners you are using.

15 Fasten the bench top to the frame with 75 mm x 10 gauge wood screws through the bench top into the top of the wall cleat and also into the tops of the legs. Make sure that the screws in the tops of the legs do not meet the screws holding the lipping to the bench top. Countersink these holes so the screw heads will be flush with the top face and use the method described in step 9 to ensure the screws are well secured in the end grain of the legs. Alternatively, the holes may be counterbored and plugged with snug plugs for a smoother bench top.

MATERIALS

TIMBER CONDITIONS

Timber is sold in three conditions:
- sawn or rough sawn: brought to a nominal size by bandsaw
- dressed all round (DAR)
- milled: dressed to a specific profile for architraves, window sills, skirting boards and so on

Sawn (nominal) size (mm)	Size after dressing (mm)
19	13
25	19
50	41
75	66
100	91
125	115
150	138
175	160
200	185
225	210
250	231
275	256
300	281

Dressed timber is sold using the same nominal dimensions as sawn timber, for example, 100 x 50 mm, but the surfaces have all been machined down to a flat, even width and thickness so that the '100 x 50 mm' timber is actually 91 x 41 mm. The table at right shows the standard sizes for seasoned timber. However, timber purchased at your local supplier may differ in actual size and this table is intended as a guide only. It is advisable to check the actual dimensions of your timber carefully before commencing work. Some measurements in the projects may need to be adjusted accordingly.

Milled timbers are also ordered by their nominal sizes. Their finished sizes will generally compare with those given in the chart for dressed timber, but check them carefully at the timber yard as there will be many variations.

Timber is usually sold in stock lengths, beginning at 1.8 m and increasing by 300 mm to 2.1 m, 2.4 m and so on. Short lengths and off-cuts may also be available.

MEDIUM DENSITY FIBREBOARD

Medium Density Fibreboard or MDF is available in standard sizes (2400 x 1200 mm is a common size) and a range of thicknesses. Your supplier or local joinery will usually be willing to cut pieces to the specific size required for your project, although there is often a small charge for this service.

MDF is suitable for indoor work that will not be exposed to the weather and it can be painted. It does, however, contain chemicals that can cause skin problems in some people. When working with MDF, always work out of the sun. Wear gloves if you have sensitive skin and protect your eyes, nose, mouth and lungs from the dust.

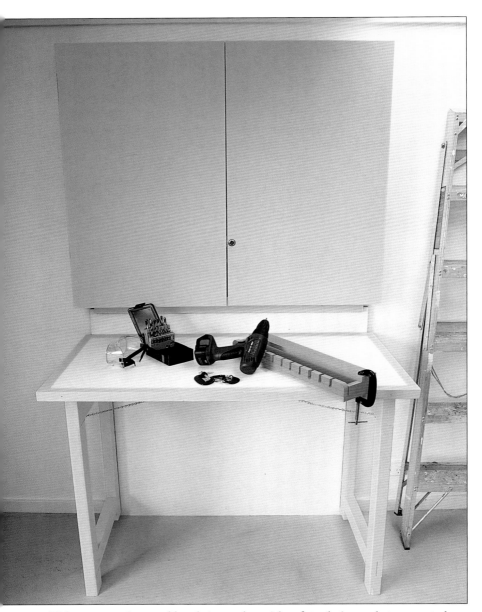

This space-saving workbench is sturdy, with safety chains and stoppers to keep the legs in the open position while you work. The lockable tool cupboard is featured on page 52.

Fold-away bench

If your workshop area is shared with other activities or even with the family car, then this bench will suit you. When not in use it folds down to take up a space of less than 100 mm from the wall.

TOOLS

- Builders square
- Pencil
- Tape measure
- Handsaw
- Three 100 mm G-cramps
- Two 1000 mm sash cramps
- Portable electric drill
- Drill bits: 4 mm, 6 mm, countersink; masonry bit (if required)
- Screwdriver (cross-head)
- Ruler or other straight edge
- Marking gauge
- Chisels: 12 mm and 18 mm bevel-edge wood chisels
- Mallet
- 200 mm shifting spanner (if required)
- Safety glasses
- Hearing protection
- Dust mask
- Gloves

FIXING THE WALL CLEAT

1 Take the two pieces of timber that will form the wall cleat and cut them both to 1100 mm long. If you want to use the lockable shadow board featured in the photograph (instructions on page 52), assemble a 'T'-shaped wall cleat. If you are only using the bench, modify the cleat to be 'L'-shaped as shown in the diagram on page 21. Glue and cramp the two pieces of the cleat together. The wall panel sits behind the lip of the cleat but is not fastened to it.

2 Check the construction of your wall and determine the type of fastenings required (see page 25). Drill suitably sized holes through the middle of the two thicknesses of timber in the wall cleat. Stand the wall panel against the wall with the long edge horizontal and position the wall cleat above it. When you are sure that it is level, insert a pencil or pointed instrument through the holes in the cleat to mark the position of the fastenings on the wall. Remove the wall cleat and drill pilot holes for the screws or wall plugs, then fasten the cleat securely to the wall.

3 Having mounted the wall cleat correctly you should be able to take hold of the wall panel close to the floor and lift it forward and out from under the wall cleat, and completely away from the wall. This enables the completed bench to become a freestanding portable bench, or to be wall-mounted, as you choose.

MATERIALS★

Part	Material	Finished length	Width	No.
Wall cleat	38 x 25 mm hardwood DAR	1100 mm		1
	75 x 25 mm hardwood DAR	1100 mm		1
Wall panel	18 mm MDF	1150 mm	1000 mm	1
Panel cleat	50 x 38 mm hardwood DAR	1200 mm		1
Top	32 mm laminated MDF	1136 mm	570 mm	1
Lipping (front)★★	38 x 38 mm solid timber DAR	1200 mm		1
Lipping (side)★★	38 x 38 mm solid timber DAR	570 mm		2
Front leg	75 x 50 mm solid pine DAR	868 mm		2
Back leg	75 x 50 mm solid pine DAR	750 mm		2
Rail	75 x 50 mm solid pine DAR	500 mm		4

OTHER: Sixty 38 mm x 12 gauge wood screws; twelve 50 mm x 12 gauge wood screws; eighty 16 mm x 8 gauge chipboard screws (or size to suit hinges); PVA adhesive; two 700 mm piano hinges; one 1100 mm piano hinge; four to six masonry bolts OR wall-fixing screws as required (see page 25); 3 mm galvanised chain or 8 mm sash cord and rubber or wooden blocks (optional)

★ Finished size: top 1200 mm x 600 mm; height (to bench top) 900 mm. Timber sizes given are nominal. For timber types and sizes see page 17.
★★ The 38 x 38 mm lipping will give a reasonable fit, though the dressed timber will be slightly narrower than the MDF. Alternatively, select 50 x 38 mm timber and dress it to the thickness of the laminated bench top, or increase the size of the MDF bench top to 1200 x 600 mm and omit the lipping entirely.

PREPARING THE WALL PANEL
4 Lay the wall panel flat on an even surface and measure 900 mm from the bottom edge. Using a pencil, square and straight edge, mark a horizontal line across the wall panel on both faces. On the back face, mark another line parallel to the first one but 16 mm below it. Along this line, mark out eight evenly spaced screw holes 160 mm apart and 15 mm from each edge. Use a 4 mm bit to drill pilot holes for the screws. Countersink the holes on the back of the panel.

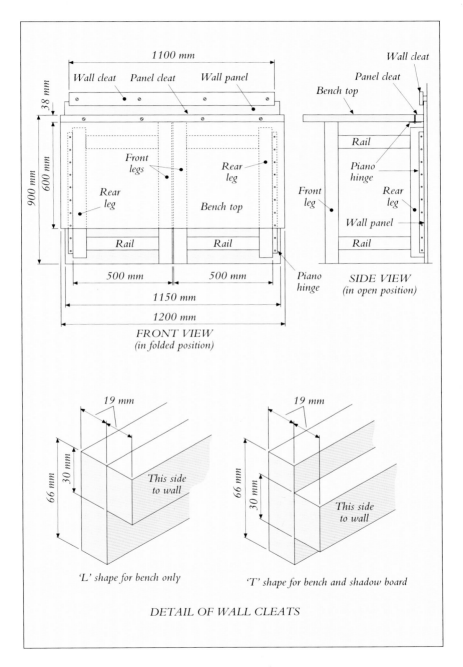

FRONT VIEW
(in folded position)

SIDE VIEW
(in open position)

'L' shape for bench only

'T' shape for bench and shadow board

DETAIL OF WALL CLEATS

21

PREPARING THE LEGS

5 Check the timber you have selected for the legs is square and measures 66 x 41 mm (dressed size). Mark off the lengths required for the front and back legs and side rails, leaving the thickness of a saw cut between each length. You will need two front legs at 868 mm each, two back legs at 750 mm each and four rails at 500 mm each.

6 Lay the front and back legs together with 66 mm faces up and the top ends of the back legs exactly 84 mm from the tops of the front legs, as indicated in the diagram opposite. Cramp them together with sash cramps or large G-cramps. Mark a line across both front legs with a pencil and square, level with the top of the back legs. Mark a second line 66 mm below this one across all four legs. Mark another line 84 mm from the bottom of the front legs, across all four legs, and a parallel line 66 mm up from this one.

7 Remove the cramps, and with the square and pencil mark the joint edge lines across the narrow sides of each leg. Set a marking gauge to half the thickness of the legs, and scribe the middle lines of the joints.

8 Lay the rails with 66 mm faces up and ends aligned and hold them together using suitable cramps. With a pencil and square, mark a line 66 mm in from each end, across all four rails. Remove the cramps and use a square and pencil to continue the joint edge lines onto the narrower faces of the rails. Use the marking gauge to scribe the joint lines around the three sides of each end.

9 Use a saw to make cuts in the waste part of the joints, cutting through the material down to the scribed centre lines. The more cuts you make, the easier it will be to remove the waste with a chisel and mallet.

10 Check the joints for fit and, if necessary, ease the shoulders with a bevel-edge chisel until the joints fit well and are square. Mark and drill pilot holes on each end of the rails, with two 38 mm x 8 gauge screws

7 Use a marking gauge set to half the thickness of the leg and rail timber to scribe the centre line for the joints.

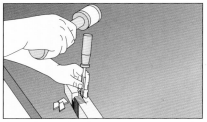

9 Make multiple saw cuts across the joint and remove the waste from the half lap joint housing.

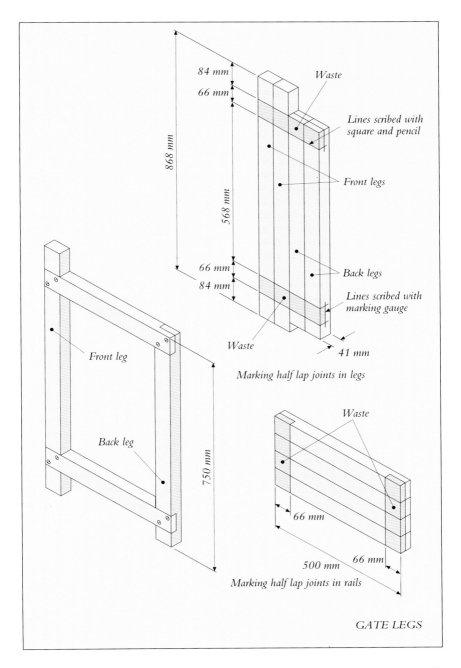

84 mm

66 mm

868 mm

568 mm

66 mm

84 mm

41 mm

Waste

Lines scribed with square and pencil

Front legs

Back legs

Lines scribed with marking gauge

Waste

Marking half lap joints in legs

Front leg

Back leg

750 mm

Waste

66 mm

66 mm

500 mm

Marking half lap joints in rails

GATE LEGS

23

The workbench and tool cupboard fold neatly against a wall, leaving the space free for other activities.

off-set diagonally for each joint. Glue and cramp the joints in place, then insert the screws.

11 Lay the wall panel on a stable, flat surface, and onto its front face lay the gate legs in closed position as shown in the plan, 95 mm from each outer edge of the wall panel. Make sure there is a gap of 10 mm between them and that they are square to the edges of the panel. Cramp them in place. Position the piano hinges and, using 16 mm x 8 gauge chipboard screws, screw the hinges to the wall panel and then to the legs. Check that the legs open easily and the wall panel and leg assembly stand square.

MAKING THE WORK TOP

12 Cut the timber lipping to size and set aside the longer (front) piece.

Take the two side pieces and determine which is the outer face of each. Mark a line with a marking gauge down the centre of these and, on this line, mark three screw holes 40 mm in from each end and in the centre. Using a 6 mm drill bit, drill and countersink holes for the 38 mm x 12 gauge wood screws. Apply adhesive to both side pieces and use sash cramps to secure them to the side edges of the bench top. Ensure that the top of the lipping is level with the laminated bench top. Repeat the process for the front lipping, with evenly spaced screw holes starting 60 mm from one end.

13 Cut the panel cleat to 1200 mm. Lay the bench top face down on a flat, level surface and lay the panel cleat along its rear edge. Position the 1100 mm piano hinge along the join and screw into place with 16 mm chipboard screws.

14 Apply a thick line of adhesive to the rear face of the panel cleat and cramp it to the front of the panel with its top aligned to the line marked at 900 mm. Firmly fix in place using 38 mm x 12 gauge screws inserted from the back.

15 Check that the legs and the top swing open easily. Fit restraints of chain or strong cord to prevent the legs being opened beyond 90 degrees and add small wooden or rubber blocks to the underside of the bench top to keep the legs open when in use.

WALL CONSTRUCTION

CONCRETE OR BRICK WALLS

These are also known as masonry walls. To make secure fastenings in these walls will involve the use of plugs or expansion bolts. Wall plugs come in various types and sizes and may be made of plastic, fibre or aluminium. The commonly used 'star plugs' are extruded plastic and come in different sizes to take different gauges of screws. You may use ordinary wood screws once the wall plugs are in place.

Expansion bolts are ideal for heavy duty purposes and operate on the same principle as wall plugs, only the plug and bolt come as a single unit. Pre-drill and countersink holes spaced evenly on the item you want to mount on the wall, then use a nail or other narrow spike to mark through the holes where you will need to drill into the masonry, being careful to avoid drilling into mortar joints or cavities. Using a masonry bit and with your portable electric drill set on low speed and hammer action, drill a hole of appropriate size in the wall to accept the plug or expansion bolt you have chosen.

TIMBER-FRAMED WALLS

First find the studs to fasten into, either by tapping with your knuckles or using an electronic stud finder. This will determine the position of the holes for the screws on the item you want to mount on the wall. If you are not sure, use a fine drill bit to drill into the wall— you will be able to feel the resistance of the timber. Mark the centres of the studs and measure the distance between them, then carefully transfer this measurement to your item. Drill and countersink the holes on the item you want to mount as usual, then insert the screws directly into the wall studs. Use 10–12 gauge wood screws at least half as long again as the thickness of timber you are fixing to the wall.

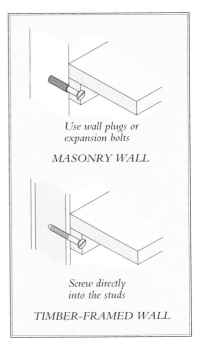

Use wall plugs or expansion bolts

MASONRY WALL

Screw directly into the studs

TIMBER-FRAMED WALL

Cabinet-makers bench

For those who are fortunate enough to have a large space in which to work and want a good size bench, this robust workbench will provide many years of service.

MATERIALS★

PART	MATERIAL	FINISHED LENGTH	NO.
Leg	200 x 38 mm solid timber DAR	860 mm	4
Top	175 x 50 mm solid timber DAR	1800 mm	6
Side rail	200 x 38 mm solid timber DAR	1800 mm	2
End rail	200 x 38 mm solid timber DAR	900 mm	2
Support rail	100 x 38 mm solid timber DAR	836 mm	2

OTHER: 50 mm x 12 gauge wood screws; twenty-four 100 mm x 12 gauge wood screws; PVA adhesive; contrasting material for plugs (19 mm solid timber DAR) or purchased 10 mm plugs; woodworking vice and stop block (optional)

★ Finished size: 1800 x 960 mm and 900 mm high. Timber sizes given are nominal. For timber types and sizes see page 17.

CONSTRUCTING THE LEGS

1 The legs are made in an 'L' shape which reduces the volume of timber (and therefore the cost) without reducing the strength. With a tape measure and pencil, mark each of the

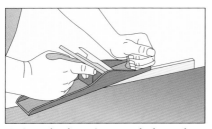

1 Cut the leg pieces and then plane the sawn edges smooth to ensure a good fit between the two pieces.

four lengths of 200 x 38 mm leg material into one 110 mm wide piece and one 75 mm wide piece (the completed leg assembly will have approximately equal sides). Rip down the length of each leg with a handsaw. Plane the sawn edges smooth and straight.

2 Draw a pencil line parallel to and 15 mm in from one edge of each of the wider pieces of timber. Mark four evenly spaced screw locations along these lines (25 mm from one end, then at 270 mm intervals) and, using a 10 mm drill bit, drill (counterbore) holes 10 mm deep.

This bench was built out of hoop pine—a stable, resilient timber of medium hardness which is cost effective for a bench of this type. The top can be re-dressed many times to counter the inevitable wear and tear.

TOOLS

- Tape measure
- Pencil
- Handsaw
- Low-angle (block) plane
- Jack plane (if required)
- Square
- Portable electric drill
- Drill bits: 6 mm, 10 mm, countersink bit
- Screwdrivers (cross-head)
- Two 100 mm G-cramps
- Two 300 mm G-cramps
- Drill stand and 10 mm plug cutter (optional)
- 18 mm bevel-edge or firmer chisel
- Mallet
- Hammer
- Safety glasses
- Dust mask
- Hearing protection

Complete the pilot holes with a 6 mm drill bit to suit the 12 gauge screws. Apply adhesive to one long edge of the 75 mm wide leg piece and cramp it against the back of the pre-drilled edge of the 110 mm wide piece. Complete the assembly by screwing in four 50 mm x 12 gauge wood screws. The counterbored holes will be plugged at a later stage.

BUILDING THE SUBFRAME

3 On a flat, smooth surface, lay out the six pieces of timber that make up the bench top and check the approximate width and length of the assembly (finished size will be 1800 x 960 mm). The final dimensions of the subframe should be the same as this measurement. Number the top pieces 1–6 with a soft pencil.

4 Cut the end rails to 900 mm (that is, the width of the bench top, less twice the thickness of the rails). On each rail, 55 mm in from the end and parallel to the end, mark a line with the pencil and square. On this line, 35 mm in from each edge, mark two screw holes, adding another in the middle. Counterbore and drill these screw holes as for the legs in step 2.

5 The solid (110 mm) face of each leg will be the end face. Determine which way is up on each leg and mark the top with a pencil mark. On each leg, 50 mm down from the top, mark a line with a square and pencil around both faces, square to the corner edge. Spread adhesive over the area of the end face where it will be covered by the rail. Align the rail with its top edge along the 50 mm line and its end aligned with the side face of the leg. Cramp it in place with 100 mm G-cramps. Insert and tighten the 50 mm x 12 gauge screws.

6 You will now have two leg/end rail assemblies. Check that the legs are square to the end rails.

7 Cut the side rails to 1800 mm (that is, the length of the bench top). On each rail, 50 mm and 100 mm in from the ends and parallel to them,

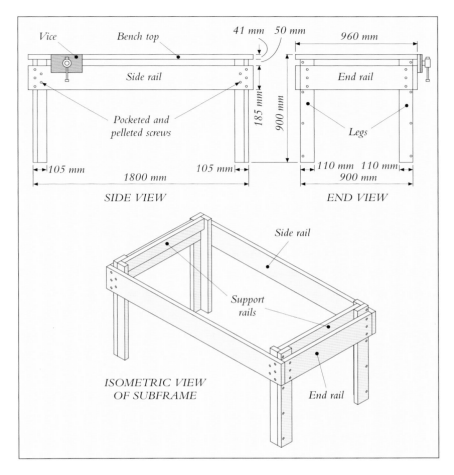

Vice Bench top 41 mm 50 mm 960 mm

Side rail End rail

Pocketed and pelleted screws

Legs

185 mm 900 mm

105 mm 1800 mm 105 mm 110 mm 110 mm 900 mm

SIDE VIEW END VIEW

Side rail

Support rails

ISOMETRIC VIEW OF SUBFRAME End rail

mark a line with the pencil and square. On the first line, 40 mm in from the top and bottom edges, mark the locations for two screw holes and add another in the centre. On the second line, mark two screw holes 60 mm in from each edge. Counterbore and drill these five screw holes as before. Apply adhesive to the area of the leg side face that will be covered by the rail, and align

the side rail upper edge to the 50 mm line marked on the leg and its end to the outer face of the end rail. Cramp it in place and insert the 50 mm x 12 gauge screws.

8 With the bench subframe complete and standing on a flat, level surface, once again check that it is absolutely square by taking measurements diagonally from each corner. If these

measurements are equal, everything is square. A small error in the order of 5–10 mm in a structure this size would be tolerable.

9 Take a measurement between the inside faces of the legs parallel to the end rails, and cut the support rails to that length, less 4 mm (approximately 836 mm). With a 6 mm twist drill, drill two evenly spaced pilot holes about 20 mm in from the edges at each end of the support rails (being careful to avoid meeting other screws already in the assembly). Apply adhesive to the inside face of the legs that will be covered by the rails. Cramp the support rails in place so that the upper edge of the rail is level with the tops of the legs and insert the 50 mm x 12 gauge wood screws.

MAKING THE BENCH TOP

10 Lay one of the bench top pieces in place so its outer edge is aligned with the outer face of the side rail, and one of its ends is aligned with the face of the end rail. Cramp it in place with 300 mm G-cramps. With a straight edge against the face of the

other end rail, mark the finished length of the top piece. Check this measurement is the same at the other side of the bench and cut all the top pieces to that length.

11 Mark a pencil line along the centre of the top edge of each of the support rails. Lay each top piece in turn in place and use a square to transfer to it the location of the support rail centre lines. On the top piece that you marked as number 1, locate a screw hole on the line so that it will be over the centre of the leg (75 mm in from the end and 45 mm in from the edge), and another hole the same distance (45 mm) from the other edge of the top piece. Repeat at the other end of the top piece. Counterbore and drill screw holes as before, then screw the timber in place with 100 mm x 12 gauge wood screws.

12 Lay out the rest of the bench top pieces and mark screw holes in the same positions as for the first piece, ensuring that the outer screw on number 6 will enter the top of the

13 Bevel any unwanted sharp edges on the bench top and subframe with a low-angle plane.

14 Use the plug cutter only in a drill stand as it is impossible to control it in a hand-held drill.

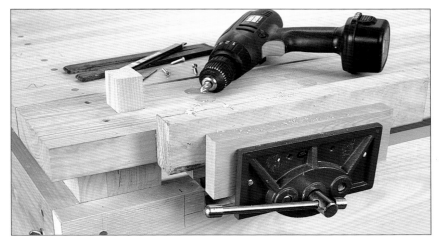

You might like to mount a vice and stop block on your bench. If necessary, cut a clearance from the side rails and hide any mounting bolts with timber plugs.

leg as for number 1. Counterbore the holes and firmly screw all pieces in place. Where the screws enter the end grain in the top of the leg, remove each screw, fill the hole with PVA adhesive and reinsert the screw to ensure a secure fastening.

FINISHING

13 Using a low-angle plane, bevel any unwanted sharp edges on the legs, rails and bench top.

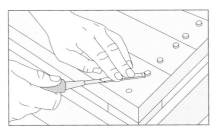

15 After the glue has set, level the plugs and trim off any excess adhesive with a firmer chisel.

14 Using a drill press and 10 mm plug cutter, cut plugs from any contrasting soft wood to cover all the external screws. A plug cutter is not suitable for a hand-held drill so, if a drill press is not available, dowel or ready-made plugs can be substituted. Apply a little PVA adhesive to each plug and, placing a piece of scrap timber over the plug to prevent damage to the work top, use a hammer to tap it in.

15 Allow a couple of hours for the adhesive to set and then trim the plugs and any excess adhesive off flush using an 18 mm firmer chisel and mallet.

16 A woodworking vice like the one shown in the photograph above is an optional accessory that many woodworkers will find useful. To

BENCH TOP WITH TOOL WELL

Old-fashioned cabinet-makers benches had a tool well—a sunken area used to prevent tools falling off the bench and being damaged (or causing damage). Many people find that the tool well becomes a receptacle for rubbish and tools that would otherwise have been cleaned up and put away, so it has been left out of the bench on page 26. However, if you want to add a tool well, this diagram shows how it may be done. When fitting the bench top as described in step 12, omit the second and third timbers, leaving a space of approximately 320 mm (the width of two top

pieces) between the first and fourth planks. Turn the bench upside down and measure the distance between the support rails, then cut two 200 x 50 mm pieces of solid timber (DAR) to that length, less 5 mm. Secure these two boards to the edges of the bench top boards with 75 mm x 10 gauge wood screws, after first gluing them together. Fit four short lengths of 175 x 50 mm timber (DAR) to fill the gaps in the bench top at the ends of the tool well, securing them with screws from the underside of the tool well and into the top of the support rail.

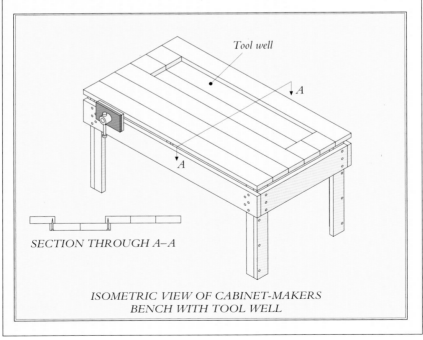

Tool well

A

A

SECTION THROUGH A–A

ISOMETRIC VIEW OF CABINET-MAKERS
BENCH WITH TOOL WELL

accommodate the permanently mounted vice, cut a clearance in the top edge piece and the side rail near one end of the bench. Counterbore and plug the holes for the bolts as for all of the other bench top screws, noting that the counterbored holes and plugs will need to be larger.

17 The adjustable stop block pictured on page 31 is fitted through the bench top just behind the support rail. Measuring 60 mm square and 300 mm long, the block is secured in the appropriate position by a bolt and wing nut. Cut a vertical slot approximately 150 mm long and the same width as the bolt in the bottom end of the block and remove one screw from the end rail to accommodate the bolt. Adjust the block as required.

USING THE BENCH TOP FOR METAL WORK

If you intend to do any metal work on your cabinet-makers bench, fit a small engineers vice with a sheet of metal underneath to prevent metal cuttings from becoming embedded in the bench top or your project.

Secure the vice with bolts through the metal plate and the bench top. Both the vice and the metal sheet can easily be unbolted and demounted from the bench when more space is required for woodwork projects.

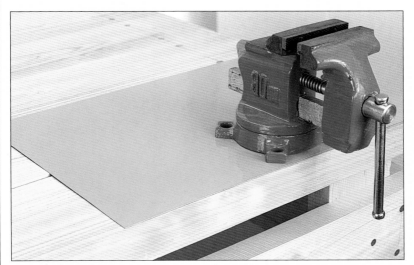

This picture shows how you may mount an engineers vice and protective metal plate on the bench. Bolt the vice securely in place before use.

The bench top is made of hoop pine and is mounted on a storage box of 16 mm MDF. If there is a gap left at the top of the drawer box, cover it with a small piece of leftover MDF, as shown here.

Bench with storage

When you have adequate floor space but wall space is at a premium, a bench top mounted on a storage cabinet may suit your needs. This storage unit has drawers and shelves and can be fitted with racks for planes, chisels and screwdrivers if desired.

ASSEMBLING THE TOP

1 Order the lengths for the bench top dressed all round, but a bit overlength. Lay them out on a flat surface and arrange the growth rings in the end grain so that they alternate as in the diagram at right.

2 The top is made in the traditional manner, by edge gluing boards together to make up the size required. Check the fit of each board with its neighbour. Ideally there should be no gaps between them, but if there are, reduce the gaps to a minimum with a jack plane, being sure to maintain the squareness of the edges. Mark the top face of each board with a soft pencil and number them 1–4.

3 Apply adhesive to each of the joining edges of the boards and bring them together without delay. Use two sash cramps under and one over to cramp the boards together. Meanwhile, with 100 mm G-cramps and some scrap timber, ensure the edges of the boards are held tightly

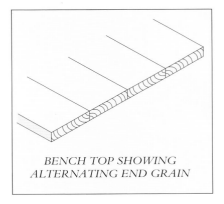

BENCH TOP SHOWING ALTERNATING END GRAIN

MATERIALS★

PART	MATERIAL	FINISHED LENGTH	WIDTH	No.
Top★★	225 x 50 mm solid timber DAR	1400 mm		4
End panel	16 mm MDF	630 mm	870 mm	2
Base panel	16 mm MDF	630 mm	1168 mm	1
Plinth (side)	16 mm MDF	630 mm	100 mm	2
Plinth (front/back)	16 mm MDF	1232 mm	100 mm	2
Mid panel	16 mm MDF	770 mm	1168 mm	1
Dividing panel	16 mm MDF	770 mm	420 mm	1
Fascia	16 mm MDF	1200 mm	75 mm	2
Front shelf	16 mm MDF	420 mm	648 mm	2
Rear shelf	16 mm MDF	1168 mm	150 mm	2
Shelf cleat	25 x 25 mm solid timber DAR	150 mm		2
Drawer side	140 x 12 mm prefabricated	400 mm		8
Drawer front/back	140 x 12 mm prefabricated	478 mm		8
Drawer base	4 mm MDF	370 mm	448 mm	4
Drawer front	16 mm MDF	520 mm	164 mm	4
Top mounting cleat	75 x 38 mm solid timber DAR	750 mm		2

OTHER: PVA adhesive; 50 mm x 8 gauge chipboard screws; forty 25 mm x 8 gauge chipboard screws for shelf supports and drawer runners; eighty 30 mm x 8 gauge chipboard screws for drawers; sixteen 20 mm x 8 gauge chipboard screws for drawer fronts; twelve 45 mm x 12 gauge wood screws for cleats; ten 10 gauge wood screws of varying lengths for bench top; twenty-four brass shelf–support plugs; four pairs of drawer runners; four drawer handles and appropriate screws; abrasive paper

★ Finished size: Bench top 1400 x 840 mm and 910 mm high; storage cabinet base 1200 x 630 mm and 870 mm high. Timber sizes given are nominal. For timber types and sizes see page 17.
★★ Timber of these dimensions (225 x 50 mm) may be hard to find and expensive, although it makes a solid and sturdy bench top. If necessary, substitute six lengths of 150 x 38 mm solid timber DAR and adjust your measurements as required.

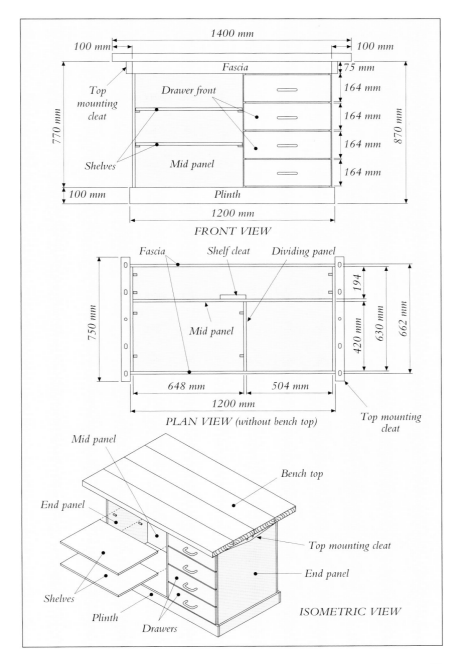

FRONT VIEW

- 1400 mm
- 100 mm
- 100 mm
- Fascia
- Top mounting cleat
- Drawer front
- 75 mm
- 164 mm
- 164 mm
- 164 mm
- 164 mm
- 770 mm
- 870 mm
- Shelves
- Mid panel
- 100 mm
- Plinth
- 1200 mm

PLAN VIEW (without bench top)

- Fascia
- Shelf cleat
- Dividing panel
- 194
- 420 mm
- 630 mm
- 662 mm
- 750 mm
- Mid panel
- 648 mm
- 504 mm
- 1200 mm
- Top mounting cleat

ISOMETRIC VIEW

- Mid panel
- Bench top
- End panel
- Top mounting cleat
- End panel
- Shelves
- Plinth
- Drawers

together with a flat profile. Tighten the sash cramps to an even pressure and remove the scrap timber before any excess adhesive causes it to stick to the bench top. Leave the bench top to dry overnight.

ASSEMBLING THE BASE

4 Your supplier will be able to cut the larger pieces of MDF to size for you or you may mark them out and cut them yourself. Take the two 630 x 870 mm pieces of MDF for the end panels of the base and measure 92 mm from the bottom edge. With a pencil and straight edge, mark a line across, parallel to the bottom edge. Along this line, mark screw holes 40 mm in from the front edge, then at 110 mm intervals (six screw holes in total). Use a 4 mm twist drill and countersink bit to drill countersunk holes from the outside face of the end panels.

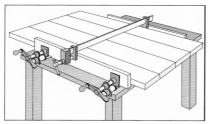

3 Use three sash cramps—two under, one over—to secure the bench top timber while the adhesive dries.

5 Cramp a straight piece of scrap timber to the inside face of each end panel so that its lower edge is exactly 100 mm from the bottom edge of the panel. Spread adhesive on one end of the 630 x 1168 mm base panel and position it against the scrap timber so that its top face is 100 mm from the lower edge of the end panel. Insert the 50 mm x 8 gauge chipboard screws from the outside face of the end panel to secure and repeat the procedure for the other end panel. Remove the scrap timber.

6 Take two 630 x 100 mm lengths of MDF for the plinth. Mark a line 8 mm down from the top of each plinth and parallel to the top edge. Mark five screw holes in each plinth piece, starting 55 mm in from one edge and then at 130 mm intervals, checking that these will not align with the positions of the screws that hold the end panels to the base. Drill and countersink the holes. Spread adhesive on the inside face of the plinth and cramp it to the lower edge of the end panel. Fasten in place with 50 mm x 8 gauge chipboard screws.

7 Take two 1232 x 100 mm lengths of MDF for the plinth and, 8 mm from the upper edge, draw a line parallel to the edge. Mark nine screw holes, starting 66 mm in from one edge, then at 140 mm intervals. On each end of the plinth, mark a screw hole 8 mm in from the end and halfway between the two edges (50 mm). Drill countersunk holes.

8 Spread adhesive on the front edge of the base panel and the lower front edges of the end panels and lay on the plinth piece, so that both ends are flush with the outer face of the side plinth pieces. The top edge of the plinth piece should be flush with the top face of the base panel. Screw into place with 50 mm x 8 gauge chipboard screws and repeat the procedure for the back plinth piece.

STORAGE MODULE

9 Check that the mid panel is a snug fit between the end panels and that its top edge aligns with the top edges of the end panels. Position the panel 420 mm in from the front edges of the end panels. With a pencil, mark lines on the end and base panels on either side of the mid panel, then remove the panel. Symmetrically mark and drill a number of screw holes (about fifteen, five on each end and five across the base) centrally between these lines. Countersink the holes from the outside face of the end panels and from underneath the base panel. Apply adhesive to the edges of the mid panel, position it between the marked lines and insert the 50 mm x 8 gauge chipboard screws to secure the panel in place.

10 Take the 420 x 770 mm dividing panel and check the fit. Mark a line square to the front edge and 504 mm from the right end panel. Align the dividing panel so its right-hand face is flush with this line, ensure that it is square with the mid panel and the

PLANE STORAGE

One drawer of the bench can be modified to store planes. Cover the bottom of the drawer with waxed baize and fasten small battens at appropriate intervals on the drawer base, to prevent your planes moving about.

base and mark lines with a pencil on both sides of the panel as you did for the mid panel in step 9. Symmetrically mark and drill approximately eight screw holes (five on the mid panel and three on the base) centrally between these lines and countersink them from the back of the mid panel and from underneath the base panel. Apply adhesive to the back and bottom edges of the dividing panel, position it between the marked lines and insert the 50 mm x 8 gauge chipboard screws to secure it.

FASCIAS AND SHELVES

11 Take the two 1200 x 75 mm fascias and cramp them to the top of the storage assembly so that the ends are flush with the outer face of the end panels on both sides. On the front piece, use a pencil to mark the position of the dividing panel and square a line across the front face of the fascia at the mid point of the dividing panel. Square a line 8 mm from each end, and on each of these three lines mark two screw holes approximately 20 mm in from each edge. Remove the fascia from the

assembly, drill and countersink the holes then, applying adhesive to the edges of the end and dividing panels where they will meet the fascia, replace it and insert the 50 mm x 8 gauge chipboard screws. Repeat at both ends of the back fascia.

12 In the end and dividing panel on the left-hand side of the module you will need to drill a series of blind holes to take the movable shelf support plugs. To ensure that the shelves are evenly spaced, cut a batten of scrap timber 770 mm long and mark a line down its centre. Mark one end of the batten as the base and mark and drill 4 mm holes right through the batten along the centre line at 200 mm from its base, then at 50 mm intervals up to 600 mm from its base. Place the batten against the end panel so the holes are approximately 100 mm in from the mid panel, ensure the batten is square to the base and drill through the holes in the batten. Fit the twist drill into the chuck so that the amount of drill protruding is equal to the thickness of the batten plus the desired depth of the blind holes (approximately 12 mm). Repeat on the dividing panel and again 100 mm in from the front of the cabinet. Cut shelves from MDF and try them to see that they fit.

13 The same scrap wood batten may be used to drill blind holes in both end panels for the narrow shelves at the rear of the storage unit. Place the batten with one edge against the mid panel and drill one set of holes, then locate the second set of holes approximately 60 mm in from the back edge of the end panels. Because of the length of these narrow shelves the 16 mm MDF is likely to bend. To prevent this, secure short lengths of 25 x 25 mm cleat to the mid panel, centrally between the end panels and with the top of the cleats in line with the top of the shelf support holes you have drilled. Use the scrap wood battens to help you mark the position of these cleats and secure them with 25 mm x 8 gauge chipboard screws.

ASSEMBLING THE DRAWERS

14 The drawers are assembled from prefabricated drawer section available from most hardware stores in 2400 mm lengths. Drawer runners are also available at most hardware stores and come in many sizes and types, so select a 400 mm runner of a type that suits your requirements. Cut eight side pieces of drawer section 400 mm long and eight front/back pieces 478 mm long. Adjust the width of the drawers if necessary to suit the type of runners you have selected, following the manufacturer's instructions. Mark and drill with a 4 mm bit four evenly spaced countersunk screw holes 6 mm in from each end of the 400 mm pieces. Partly assemble a drawer body and check the size of the drawer base before cutting four bases from 4 mm MDF.

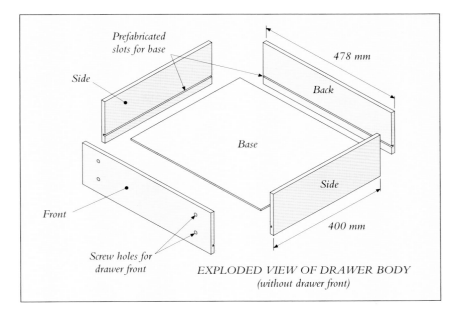

Prefabricated slots for base

Side

Back

478 mm

Base

Side

Front

400 mm

Screw holes for drawer front

EXPLODED VIEW OF DRAWER BODY
(without drawer front)

15 Apply adhesive to the ends of the side pieces and assemble the drawer bodies, inserting the bases into the prefabricated slots before fitting in the fourth side. Use 30 mm x 8 gauge screws to secure. Once the drawer is assembled, remove one screw at a time, insert adhesive in the hole and replace the screw, tightening firmly but being careful not to over tighten the screws.

16 Following the manufacturer's instructions, attach the drawer runners to the inside of the cabinet with centres approximately 168 mm apart. Attach the remaining runner hardware to each drawer body, following the manufacturer's instructions, in readiness for fitting the drawer into the cabinet.

17 Mark and drill two screw holes approximately 60 mm in from each end and 60 mm apart on the inside of the front panel. Countersink the holes on the inside. Cut four drawer fronts from 16 mm MDF, each measuring 520 mm by 164 mm.

18 Mount the bottom drawer body on its runners and position a drawer

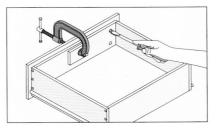

18 Cramp the first drawer front to the body and insert the screws from the inside of the drawer.

front with an 8 mm overlap on each side edge and a couple of millimetres clearance from the base of the cabinet. Use 100 mm G-cramps to cramp the front to the body before withdrawing the assembly and drilling pilot holes for the 20 mm x 8 gauge chipboard screws. Securely screw the drawer front to the body.

19 Return the completed drawer to the cabinet and position the next drawer above it. Allowing a 3–4 mm gap between the drawer fronts, cramp the next drawer front to the body and assemble as before. To attach the top drawer front, partially screw the holding screws through the front of the drawer body so the points project outwards slightly and press the MDF front against the screws to mark the correct positions. Drill pilot holes in the MDF, then remove the top drawer body from the cabinet to attach the drawer front. When all fronts are attached, mark and drill the positions for the drawer handles, drilling right through the drawer front and body. Firmly screw the handles in place.

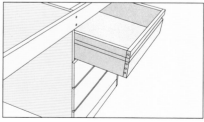

19 Return each completed drawer to the cabinet to give the correct position for the MDF front of the drawer above.

ADDING THE TOP

20 Take the two top mounting cleats and taper the edges if you like, as shown in the diagram opposite. Cut away the waste with a saw and dress the sawn faces with a plane, rounding over the ends at the same time. Mark holes with centres approximately 35 mm from each end of the cleat, then at 170 mm intervals (this will place one hole directly in the centre of the cleat). These holes should be drilled vertical to the top edge of the cleat and all except the centre hole must be elongated to allow for the expansion and contraction of the timber top. Use a 5 mm twist drill to make two pilot holes, one either side of the centres you have marked, then remove any material between the two holes with a very fine chisel. Counterbore the holes to a depth of around 5 mm using a 10 mm twist drill and making elongated holes as before.

21 The cleats are attached to the end panels with adhesive and 45 mm x 12 gauge wood screws. The holes for the screws that fasten these cleats to the MDF panelling should be countersunk on the inner face of the end panels. Mark screw holes at 60 mm from each end of the panel and also at 170 mm from each end and 280 mm from each end. Cramp the cleat to the end panel and ensure that the marked screw holes will not interfere with the counterbored holes for the top fastening screws. Drill pilot holes with a 6 mm drill bit.

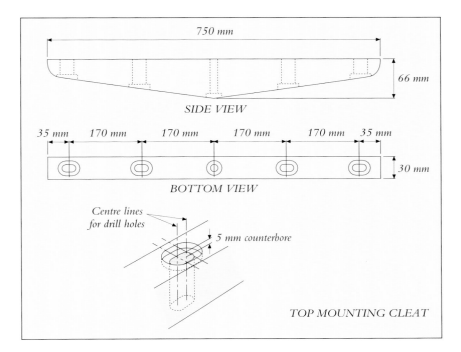

Apply adhesive to the inner face of the cleat and cramp it to the end panel. Insert the screws.

22 Allow the adhesive holding the cleats to the cabinet to dry, preferably overnight. Once the adhesive has set, lay the bench top on the MDF cabinet and align it square. Use 10 gauge wood screws that are approximately 15 mm longer than the depth of the pilot holes in the cleat; that is, two 40 mm screws at each end, two 50 mm screws and one 60 mm screw in the centre. Insert the screws centrally in the elongated slots and screw the top down firmly. Check that all is square, then loosen each screw off by half a

turn. Do not use adhesive to secure the bench top to the cabinet.

23 Use a saw and plane to level the ends of the top timbers and slightly bevel all edges with a block plane. A little sanding here and there may be needed to create a pleasing finish.

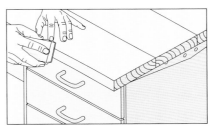

23 Once the workbench is complete, plane the ends of the bench top square and finish with a little sanding.

Plane rack

This rack can be fixed to almost any vertical surface—a wall, the end of a workbench or a shadow board—and will keep your planes conveniently at hand. The shelves will fit planes up to 450 mm long (a No. 6).

MATERIALS★				
PART	MATERIAL	FINISHED LENGTH	WIDTH	NO.
Back board	16 mm MDF	500 mm	420 mm	1
Bottom shelf	16 mm MDF	500 mm	90 mm	1
Upper shelf	16 mm MDF	500 mm	70 mm	2
Lipping	31 x 19 mm solid timber DAR	420 mm		3

OTHER: Sixteen 30 mm x 8 gauge chipboard screws; nine 20 mm x 1 mm panel pins; PVA adhesive; adhesive-backed baize; furniture wax

★ Finished size: 420 x 500 mm and 120 mm deep. Timber sizes given are nominal. For timber types and sizes see page 17.

CUTTING OUT THE PIECES

1 On a piece of 16 mm MDF, mark out the dimensions of the back board and use a handsaw to cut it out. Cut on the waste side of your pencil marks and plane the edges straight and smooth. The rounded top corners are optional but give a nice finish. Use a jar lid or round template to trace the shape, cutting away the waste with a saw and smoothing with a file.

2 Similarly, mark out and cut the three shelves to the sizes indicated in the materials list and plane the edges smooth and square. Again, the rounded corners are optional, and are created using the same template as for the back board.

3 Take the timber battens for the lipping and mark off three 420 mm lengths, allowing a few millimetres space for the saw cut in between

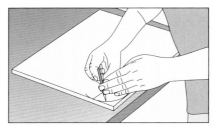

1 The round corners are created by using a compass or curved template such as a jar lid to trace the shape.

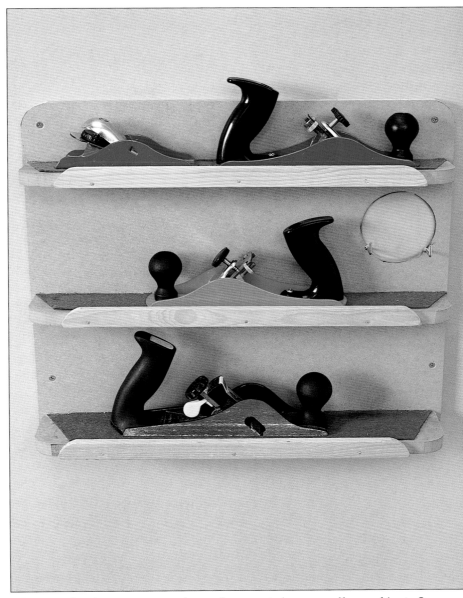

This simple plane storage rack can be mounted on a wall or cabinet. In addition to the planes, it has space for a traditional home-made waxing tin to lubricate the sole plates of the planes before use.

TOOLS

- Builders square and pencil
- Tape measure
- Handsaw
- Smoothing plane
- Second-cut file
- Portable electric drill
- Drill bits: 4 mm, countersink, masonry bit (if required)
- Two 100 mm G-cramps
- Scissors
- Hammer
- Dust mask
- Safety glasses
- Hearing protection

file—it is not necessary to use a template for these small curves.

ADDING THE SHELVES

4 On the back face of the back board, 8 mm up from the lower edge, mark a line parallel to that edge. Mark four screw holes along this line, the first 15 mm from the side edge, then at 140 mm intervals. Drill and countersink the holes with a 4 mm drill bit suitable for the 30 mm x 8 gauge chipboard screws.

5 To position the other shelves, measure up 160 mm from the first line and mark and drill countersunk screw holes as for the bottom shelf. Measure 160 mm from this line and repeat the process. Note: using these measurements, the top shelf will be approximately 80 mm from the top

each length. Cut each piece to length with a handsaw, then simply round the top corners off with a second-cut

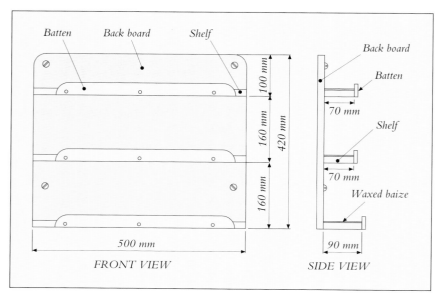

FRONT VIEW   SIDE VIEW

edge of the back board. This should accommodate a low-angle plane and a No. 3 smoothing plane.

6 On the front face of the rack, measure 160 and 320 mm from the bottom edge and mark the positions of the shelves, 8 mm below the pilot holes for the screws. Drill pilot holes in the back edge of each shelf to correspond with the positions of the pilot holes in the back board. Apply adhesive to the back edges of the shelves, cramp them in place with their bottom faces aligned with the base of the back panel and the marked lines, and screw them in place using 30 mm x 8 gauge chipboard screws.

FINISHING

7 Using scissors, cut three lengths of adhesive-backed baize 450 mm long and 70 mm wide. Peel off the backing paper and apply it to the top face of each shelf. Trim the baize at the front corners with scissors and verly lightly wax the baize using furniture wax. The waxed baize is intended to keep the sole plates from rusting, and the minuscule amount of wax that adheres to the sole will help the plane glide over your work.

8 Centre the wooden battens on the front of each shelf and ensure that the bottom edge of the batten is flush with the bottom of the shelf. Use three 20 mm x 1 mm panel pins to secure the batten to the front of each shelf. This will prevent the planes falling off the rack.

9 To hang the plane rack on a wall or the side of your workbench, drill four countersunk screw holes through the back board. Position a screw approximately 25 mm from each top corner and the other two screws approximately half-way between the bottom shelf and the second shelf. If you are attaching the rack to a storage cupboard or shadow board made of MDF or similar, 30 mm x 8 gauge chipboard screws will be sufficient. If hanging the rack directly on a wall, use fasteners suitable for the wall construction and alter the position of the screw holes if necessary (see page 25).

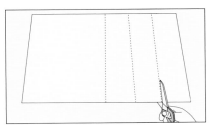

7 Use scissors to cut the baize to size, trimming the corners to shape after it has been applied to the shelves.

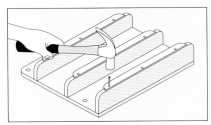

8 Hammer 20 mm panel pins through the lipping battens to secure them to the front of the shelves.

Chisels and other sharp-edged tools should not be loosely stored together, to prevent damage to the tools' edges and the user's hands. These two simple projects, mounted on a wall or workbench, can be an effective storage solution.

Chisel and screwdriver racks

These simple racks can be fastened to almost any vertical surface so that your hand tools are always close by and safely stored.

TOOLS

- Tape measure
- Builders square and pencil
- Handsaw
- Marking gauge
- Portable electric drill
- Twist drills: 4 mm, 10 mm, 12 mm, 15 mm, countersink bit
- Two 100 mm G-cramps
- Screwdriver (cross-head)
- Dust mask
- Safety glasses
- Hearing protection

CHISEL RACK

1 Mark out all pieces of the chisel rack to the sizes described in the materials list on a piece of 16 mm MDF, remembering to leave a 3 or 4 mm cutting space between the pieces. Cut out the pieces using a handsaw. Rounding the corners of the 550 x 44 mm rack top is optional.

2 On the rack top, use a marking gauge to scribe a line 25 mm in from the front edge and parallel to it. Starting 50 mm in from one end of the rack top, mark off 45 mm sections by drawing a line with a pencil and square across the top face. Where the lines intersect, drill holes

with a 10, 12, or 15 mm drill bit to fit your chisel shanks.

3 From the sides of each drilled hole to the front edge of the rack, use a square and pencil to mark two parallel lines approximately 8–12 mm apart. Cut along these lines with a handsaw and discard the waste.

4 On the back face of the back board, mark a line 8 mm from the top edge and parallel to it. Mark five evenly spaced screw holes along this line. On each side of the back board, 8 mm in from the edge, mark two screw holes approximately 40 mm from the top and bottom edges. With a 4 mm twist drill, drill pilot holes and countersink them.

5 Spread adhesive on the back edge of the top, cramp it at right angles to the

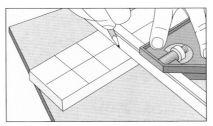

2 Mark lines at 45 mm intervals along the rack top to intersect the lengthwise line.

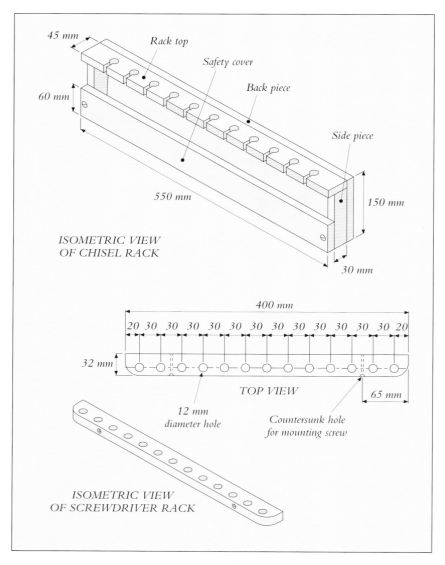

45 mm

Rack top

Safety cover

Back piece

60 mm

Side piece

550 mm

150 mm

ISOMETRIC VIEW
OF CHISEL RACK

30 mm

400 mm

20 30 30 30 30 30 30 30 30 30 30 30 30 20

32 mm

TOP VIEW

65 mm

12 mm
diameter hole

Countersunk hole
for mounting screw

ISOMETRIC VIEW
OF SCREWDRIVER RACK

top of the back board, drill pilot holes
and insert the 38 mm x 8 gauge
chipboard screws. Repeat the gluing,
cramping and screwing process for the
two side pieces.

6 Mark a screw hole in each end of
the front face of the safety cover.
Locate this hole 8 mm in from the
edge and halfway (30 mm) from the
top and bottom edges. Drill and

MATERIALS★

Part	Material	Finished length	Width	No.
Chisel rack back board	16 mm MDF	550 mm	150 mm	1
Chisel rack top	16 mm MDF	550 mm	45 mm	1
Chisel rack side piece	16 mm MDF	120 mm	30 mm	2
Chisel rack safety cover	16 mm MDF	550 mm	60 mm	1
Screwdriver rack	16 mm MDF	400 mm	32 mm	1

OTHER: Fifteen 38 mm x 8 gauge chipboard screws for chisel rack; two 50 mm x 8 gauge chipboard screws for screwdriver rack; PVA adhesive

★ Finished size: Chisel rack: 550 x 150 mm and 62 mm deep; Screwdriver rack: 400 mm long and 32 mm deep

countersink the holes. Apply adhesive to the lower front edges of the side pieces and cramp the safety cover in place. Insert the screws.

7 To hang the rack, drill and countersink two holes in the back panel. Chipboard screws will be fine if you are attaching the rack to an MDF storage cupboard or shadow board. If you are hanging the rack on a wall, select the appropriate fasteners (see page 25).

SCREWDRIVER RACK

8 Take the 400 x 32 mm piece of MDF and slightly round the two front corners if desired. This size rack holds up to thirteen screwdrivers but can be made to hold more by increasing the length appropriately. Allow an extra 30 mm per screwdriver.

9 Using a marking gauge, scribe a line 12 mm from the front edge and parallel to it. Use a square and pencil

to mark transverse lines across the piece 20 mm from one end, then at 30 mm increments. Where the lines intersect, use a 12 mm drill bit to drill holes through the rack.

10 The rack can be simply mounted on the wall by drilling two screw holes through the front edge and countersinking them. Position them between the second and third holes from each end of the rack (65 mm from each end). Use 50 mm x 8 gauge chipboard screws to fasten the rack to a wall or vertical surface.

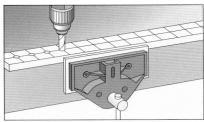

9 Drill holes with an electric drill and a 12 mm drill bit at the points where the marked lines intersect.

Small lockable shadow board

In a shared work space a small wall-mounted lockable cupboard is a great idea for storing tools. The one shown here is ideal for mounting above a workbench.

MATERIALS*

PART	MATERIAL	FINISHED LENGTH	WIDTH	NO.
Back panel	16 mm MDF	1200 mm	1000 mm	1
Side panel	16 mm MDF	1000 mm	100 mm	2
Top/bottom/shelf	16 mm MDF	1168 mm	100 mm	3
Door	16 mm MDF	1000 mm	598 mm	2
Stiffening cleat	50 x 25 mm timber DAR	1168 mm		2

OTHER: Forty 50 mm x 10 gauge chipboard screws; two 710 mm piano hinges; twenty 16 mm x 8 gauge chipboard screws or appropriate size for piano hinges; PVA adhesive; six 25 mm x 10 gauge wood screws; six mounting screws or bolts to suit wall type; two brass barrel bolts and suitable screws; locking mechanism and suitable screws; hooks, eyes, brackets appropriate for your tools; paint and pencil for shadows (optional)

* Finished size: 1000 x 1200 mm and 132 mm deep. Timber sizes given are nominal. For timber types and sizes see page 17.

PREPARING THE PIECES

1 Cut the MDF panels to the sizes indicated and plane the edges smooth and square. Alternatively, your supplier may be able to cut the pieces to size for you when you purchase your materials.

2 On the back face of the back panel, draw lines parallel to the edges 8 mm in from each side edge and the top edge. Do the same 28 mm and 194 mm up from the bottom edge. Mark six screw holes along each horizontal line, starting 75 mm in from the edge and continuing at 210 mm intervals. Mark five screw holes along the two vertical lines, beginning 100 mm from the top edge and continuing at 200 mm intervals. With a 5 mm bit, drill the holes and countersink them from the back face of the panel.

3 Take both 1000 x 100 mm side panel pieces and identify the inner face and the top end with suitable markings. Using a square, mark a line

Almost all types of hand tools can be mounted on a shadow board. The fact that this one is lockable is useful for security and for ensuring a neat and tidy appearance in a workshop that may be shared with other activities.

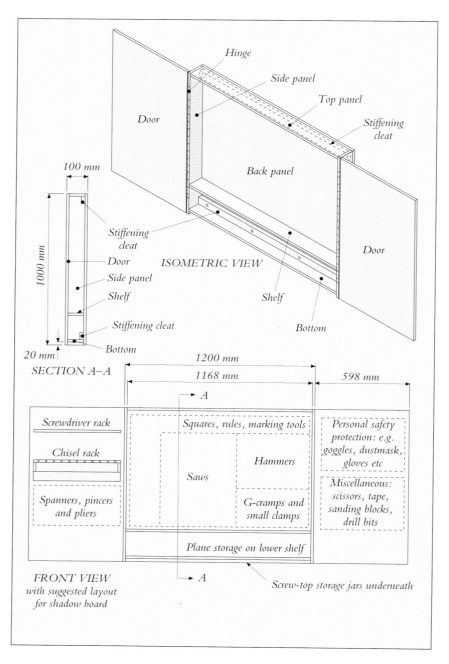

Hinge

Side panel

Top panel

Stiffening
cleat

Door

Back panel

Door

100 mm

Stiffening
cleat

1000 mm

Door

Side panel

Shelf

Shelf

ISOMETRIC VIEW

Stiffening cleat

Bottom

20 mm

Bottom

SECTION A–A

1200 mm

1168 mm

598 mm

A

Screwdriver rack

Squares, rules, marking tools

Personal safety
protection: e.g.
goggles, dustmask,
gloves etc

Chisel rack

Hammers

Miscellaneous:
scissors, tape,
sanding blocks,
drill bits

Saws

Spanners, pincers
and pliers

G-cramps and
small clamps

Plane storage on lower shelf

FRONT VIEW
with suggested layout
for shadow board

A

Screw-top storage jars underneath

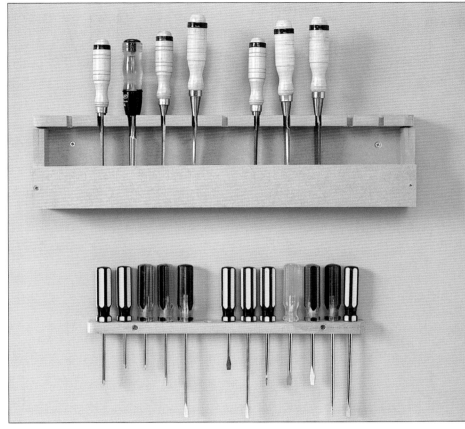

A collection of well-maintained hand tools is the basis of your workshop. Buy tools as you need them to ensure that they are exactly right for the job.

- 60/30 degree set square
- 45 degree protractor
- 180 degree protractor
- Clutch pencil, leads and eraser
- Sliding bevel gauge
- Mitre gauge
- 600 mm rule
- Mortice gauge
- Dovetail gauge
- Dovetail saw

- G-cramps, various sizes
- Cabinet-makers scraper
- Wood chisels (8, 16, 20 mm)
- Complete set of twist drills
- Pincers
- Staple gun
- Pin hammer
- Long-nose pliers
- Complete screwdriver set
- Web clamps

Fixed machinery

The following fixed power tools are among the most frequently used in a do-it-yourself workshop. While they make some jobs easier, anything these machines can do may also be done with well-maintained hand tools and a little more time and effort.

There is an ill-advised tendency for some beginners to rush out and buy fancy gleaming machines so they can do the job easier and better. The beginner may also take advice from well-meaning friends and eager salesmen that this machine, or that, is a definite 'must have'. Nothing could be further from the truth.

There are many classes and small schools operated by reputable woodworkers, and beginners should avail themselves of these services. These classes will stress the vital safety precautions to be taken when using woodworking tools, especially fixed machines. Highly detailed advice will be given about eye and hearing protection, together with instruction in the correct use of face masks for respiratory protection against airborne dusts and fumes.

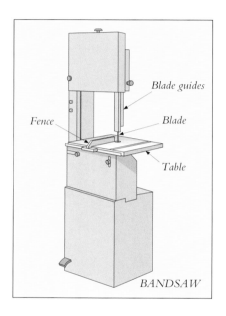

BANDSAW

BANDSAW

The need for a bandsaw will be felt, early on, by most beginners, and the purchase of a suitable machine must be given serious thought. The bandsaw is an upright saw with a narrow steel blade, able to make curved as well as straight cuts. Bandsaws are usually referred to by the diameter of the wheels and the most suitable size for the hobbyist woodworker is a two-wheel machine with 300 mm wheels. Reputable manufacturers will usually supply an owner's handbook, which will deal with the adjustment of the machine and the many safety aspects, but without very much information about the use of the saw itself.

Beginners woodworking classes or expert private tuition are the best ways to learn how to correctly and safely use a bandsaw.

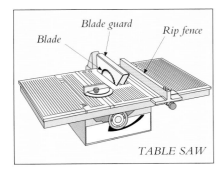

Blade

Blade guard

Rip fence

TABLE SAW

TABLE SAW

Table saws are often high on the beginner's 'want list' and here, too, great care and restraint must be exercised. These machines, in the hands of an experienced operator, are an extremely versatile tool. Used by the inexperienced these saws can, and do, become lethal weapons. The exacting adjustment of the table saw's various components is vital for the safe and efficient use of the table saw.

Table saws vary greatly in size, from tiny machines with 100 mm diameter saws as used by miniaturists to the monsters seen in sawmills. The one best suited to the beginner would have a blade of about 250 mm diameter. Freestanding models are

available but a benchtop version will meet the needs of most hobbyists.

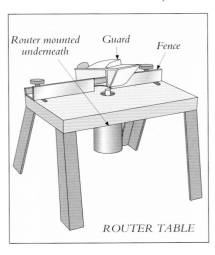

Router mounted underneath

Guard

Fence

ROUTER TABLE

ROUTER TABLE

The advent of the router and its improved affordability has made the life of the hobbyist woodworker much more interesting. It is a very versatile tool, and in the freehand mode it is possibly as safe as a woodworking machine can be. The router can be used freehand with suitable fences and bearing-guided cutters to do the jobs of many other workshop tools, such as planing, shaping and even sawing.

Today, routers are often mounted under a table top, with the cutter projecting above the table top. With fences and guides it becomes a very useful machine. Known in this form as a table router, the increase in the danger factor is possibly tenfold. It becomes, in effect, a miniature version of the industrial machine known as a spindle mounter, which is considered by many to be the most dangerous woodworking machine of all. If you are a novice in the use of a router you would be well advised to take lessons before purchasing one for your workshop.

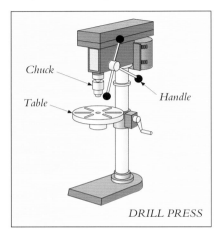

Chuck

Table

Handle

DRILL PRESS

90 degrees either side of the centre line. The work piece can be firmly held to the table with clamps, which allows the drilling to be controlled with great accuracy and versatility.

Always follow the drill press manufacturer's instructions regarding the speed of the drill for different materials you may be using and exercise the same care as you would with your portable drill.

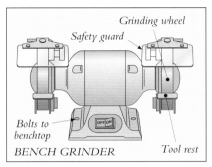

Grinding wheel

Safety guard

Bolts to benchtop

BENCH GRINDER

Tool rest

DRILL PRESS

Drill presses have become almost irreplaceable in the hobbyist workshop and are relatively safe if the necessary precautions are understood and followed.

The drill press is usually bench mounted, but large floor-standing versions are available. The drill bit is held in a chuck attached to the lower end of a revolving shaft which can be raised and lowered by a handle projecting from the side of the machine frame. The machine is fitted with a table that is adjustable vertically and horizontally about the machine's vertical circular support column and can be tilted in excess of

BENCH GRINDER

The bench grinder is an important tool and it is relatively safe if the necessary safety procedures are followed. The bench grinder consists of an electric motor with a shaft at each end. These shafts are fitted with grinding wheels which enable you to keep your tools in good condition, ultimately saving you money and making your work easier.

The machine will be fitted with adjustable tool rests and toughened glass safety screens. The tool rests should be adjusted very close to the spinning wheels so your work piece cannot become jammed between the tool rest and the spinning wheel—a very dangerous thing to happen. The wheels must run true, and there are dressing tools or stones for this task. If a wheel becomes chipped, cracked or damaged in any way it must be discarded immediately.

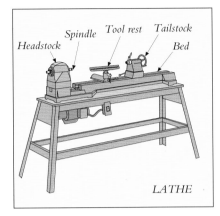

Headstock *Spindle* *Tool rest* *Tailstock* *Bed*

LATHE

LATHE

The wood lathe is a very popular machine and is available in a bewildering range of styles and sizes. The lathe is used to hold and turn a piece of wood while a cutting tool such as a gauge or scraper chisel or parting tool creates details in a piece of timber. It is used to make round things of extraordinary variety and artistry. When choosing a lathe, check that the clearance between the headstock and the bed of the lathe is adequate for the diameter of the work you intend to do on it.

Special tools are needed for woodturning and classes to instruct you in the skills and methods required to make turned projects are frequently offered.

SAFETY TIPS

You may already be familiar with these machines and their uses, but it is important not to allow familiarity to lead to unsafe working practices.

● When using any piece of machinery, fixed or hand–held, follow the manufacturer's instructions at all times and always make sure you understand the correct safety procedures.

● Never attempt to fix or modify any of these machines yourself. Contact a qualified electrician or the manufacturer's representative to carry out any repairs or adjustments that are not covered in the owner's manual.

● Use fences and safety guards whenever they are fitted. Refer to the machine owner's manual for their correct adjustment.

● Always use safety glasses and hearing protection when using fixed machinery and be alert for possible hazards such as dust, loose clothing or long hair.

● For best results when using a bandsaw, keep the blade guides close to the work piece.

● Use a push stick, not your fingers, to guide work pieces through a table saw and to clear material away from the blade.

● Remove as much waste timber as you can from your work piece before using a shaping tool such as a router or lathe.

Index